SKEWERED

SATAYS, BROCHETTES and KEBABS
SKEWERED
ELSA PETERSEN-SCHEPELERN

photography by
WILLIAM LINGWOOD

RYLAND
PETERS
& SMALL

Designer	Paul Tilby
Food Editor	Elsa Petersen-Schepelern
Editor	Maddalena Bastianelli
Production	Patricia Harrington
Head of Design	Gabriella Le Grazie
Publishing Director	Anne Ryland
Food Stylist	Bridget Sargeson
Stylist	Helen Trent

Acknowledgements

Particular thanks to Shona Adhikari and Chef Manjit Gill of Delhi's Bokhara Restaurant in the Maurya Sheraton Hotel for unlocking the secrets of successful tandoori cooking. My thanks to my sister Kirsten, to my nephews Peter Bray and Luc Votan (for his expert advice on Vietnamese food) and to friend and food writer Clare Ferguson for her Paprika Chicken. Thanks also to Helen, Bridget and Norah for beautiful props and delicious food styling, to Paul Tilby for his splendid design (as usual) and to William Lingwood for his wonderful photographs.

First published in Great Britain in 2000
10 9 8 7 6 5 4 3 2 1

by Ryland Peters & Small, Cavendish House,
51–55 Mortimer Street, London W1N 7TD

Text © Elsa Petersen-Schepelern 2000
Design and photographs © Ryland Peters & Small 2000

Printed and bound in China by Toppan Printing Co.

ISBN 1 84172 008 9

A CIP record for this book is available from the British Library.

Notes

All spoon measurements are level unless otherwise stated.

Barbecues, ovens and grills should be heated to the required temperature before adding the food.

Specialist Asian ingredients are available in large supermarkets, Thai, Chinese, Japanese and Vietnamese shops, as well as Asian stores.

CONTENTS

SATAYS, BROCHETTES, KEBABS
and SPIEDINI

Around the world, cooks and chefs have devised interesting and delicious ways to prepare foods to be cooked on skewers. It makes a small quantity go a long way – and allows marinades and other flavourings to penetrate further into the main ingredients. (All those toasty barbecued edges are a bonus.)

Cher's character in the movie *Mermaids* must be the patron saint of food on sticks. She was incapable of serving ordinary food, only amazing concoctions of multiple ingredients on skewers. However I think the fewer ingredients on a stick, the better. Each one cooks at a different rate, so my idea of hell is to have well-cooked meat interspersed with half-raw peppers and onions – or the opposite; perfectly cooked vegetables and meat burnt to a cinder. But, if you must mix them, part-cook firmer ingredients before threading and limit yourself to just a few kinds.

When you've threaded the skewers, you can leave them, covered with marinade and foil or a lid, for an hour or two in the refrigerator. Acidic ingredients such as vinegar, tomatoes or lemon juice will help preserve the food a little, as well as tenderizing and flavouring it. (But don't wait around – cook them as quickly as possible!)

Preparing your barbecue   If you're cooking on a barbecue (a traditional stick-cooking method) take care to prepare it properly. Methods vary, according to the kind of barbecue, but in general, before you start to cook, the coals should be ash-grey, radiating heat with no flame visible, otherwise the food will be charcoal outside and raw inside. Start the fire 30–45 minutes before you plan to cook. To make sure that food, especially chicken and pork, is well cooked, space the pieces well apart on the stick – or, if you like rare beef or lamb, clump the chunks together on the stick.

Preparing the skewers   If using wooden skewers, always soak them in water for at least 30 minutes first, to stop them bursting into flames.

Other cooking methods   If you don't have a barbecue, you can still skewer! A grill, stove-top grill pan (sometimes called a griddle) or an oven will all work well – just heat them to grilling speed first.

As a true pumpkin aficionado, I am picky about my pumpkins. I don't approve of the watery-fleshed kind with brown or orange skins. It has to be blue-grey or green for me, having been brought up with an Australian variety called the Queensland Blue. This type has a good, firm texture, suitable for skewering, plus wonderful taste and brilliant colour.

PUMPKIN, SWEET POTATO
and SWEET PEPPER KEBABS

2 ORANGE OR RED PEPPERS, HALVED AND DESEEDED

500 g PEELED AND DESEEDED FIRM-FLESHED PUMPKIN

500 g PEELED ORANGE SWEET POTATO

OLIVE OIL OR MUSTARD OIL, FOR BRUSHING

BLACK SEEDS, LIGHTLY BRUISED, FROM 6 GREEN CARDAMOM PODS

SEA SALT AND FRESHLY GROUND BLACK PEPPER

About 8 metal or bamboo skewers (if bamboo, soak in water for 30 minutes)

SERVES 4

Char-grill the halved peppers until the skin blisters, then put in a saucepan and cover tightly. Let steam for 10 minutes, then scrape off the skin. Cut the peppers into 2.5 cm squares and the pumpkin and sweet potato into 2.5 cm cubes, then thread them alternately onto the skewers.

Brush the vegetables with olive oil or mustard oil and cook on a barbecue or under the grill for about 15 minutes until cooked through and browned at the edges. (Half way through the cooking time, sprinkle with the cardamom seeds.) Test for tenderness and cook for 5 minutes longer if necessary*.

Serve with meat or poultry or, for vegetarians, on a bed of beans.

Note: To save time, the pumpkin and sweet potato may be par-boiled for 5 minutes before threading.

VEGETABLES

AUBERGINE and CHEESE BROCHETTES
with TOMATO and ROSEMARY SALSA

It's very important to cook aubergines properly and, since they will take longer to cook than than the cheese, they should be part-cooked before threading. Baby aubergines, unlike some of the modern hothouse varieties, still retain the tendency to bitterness and should be salted before cooking. You should slice them, sprinkle with salt and set aside for about 30 minutes. Rinse and pat dry before cooking. Salting vegetables like aubergines, cucumbers and courgettes also removes some of the water, softens the flesh and intensifies the flavour. Choose a cheese that doesn't melt easily, like Greek haloumi, Indian paneer or Italian provolone.

Using a mandoline or sharp knife, slice the aubergines thinly lengthways. Salt, rinse and pat dry as described in the recipe introduction. Preheat a stove-top grill pan, brush with oil, add the aubergine slices and char-grill on both sides until almost completely cooked, pressing down with a spatula as you do, so the flesh is marked in lines.

Remove and cool a little. Do the same to the slices of cheese, browning them on all sides. Cut into 2.5 cm squares, thread onto skewers, threading the aubergine zig-zag fashion around the cheese.

Mix the honey with the lime juice and salt and brush the brochettes on all sides. Grill until the edges are crisp.

Mix the salsa ingredients together and serve with the skewers and yoghurt, if using.

8 BABY AUBERGINES (FROM AN ASIAN MARKET), OR 2 LONG, THIN AUBERGINES

OLIVE OIL, FOR BRUSHING

250 g NON-MELTING CHEESE SUCH AS GREEK HALOUMI, ITALIAN PROVOLONE OR INDIAN PANEER, CUT INTO 1 cm SLICES

3 tablespoons HONEY, WARMED

FRESHLY SQUEEZED JUICE OF 3 LIMES

SEA SALT AND FRESHLY GROUND BLACK PEPPER

250 ml GREEK OR PLAIN YOGHURT, TO SERVE (OPTIONAL)

TOMATO AND ROSEMARY SALSA

4 MEDIUM TOMATOES, COARSELY CHOPPED

1 tablespoon CHOPPED FRESH ROSEMARY LEAVES, PLUS 4 SMALL SPRIGS, TO SERVE

8 metal or bamboo skewers, (if bamboo, soak in water for at least 30 minutes)

SERVES 4

20–24 BABY POTATOES, ABOUT 2.5 cm DIAMETER

4–8 SPRIGS OF ROSEMARY, ABOUT 15 cm LONG

OLIVE OIL, FOR BRUSHING

SEA SALT AND FRESHLY GROUND BLACK PEPPER

1 metal kebab skewer

strips of foil for wrapping leaves

SERVES 4

Wash the potatoes well, then spin them dry in a salad spinner (this will roughen the surface, giving a more crunchy exterior).

Par-boil the potatoes in salted water for 10 minutes. Drain, plunge into cold water, then pierce through with a metal skewer.

Trim the rosemary sprigs so the woody part is smooth and just a few leaves remain attached at the end. Wrap the leaves in a twist of foil.

Remove the skewer and replace with a trimmed rosemary sprig, threading 3–5 potatoes on each one.* Brush with oil, sprinkle with salt and pepper and cook under a hot grill or on the barbecue for about 10–15 minutes, turning once, or until cooked through and well browned.

***Note:** The sticks can be prepared ahead to this point.*

ITALIAN POTATOES
on ROSEMARY STICKS

Woody herbs like bay and rosemary can be used as skewers for meats and vegetables, giving gorgeous flavour to the whole dish. They are especially good with lamb, the natural companion for rosemary.

CHAR-GRILLED SUGAR-GLAZED CHERRY TOMATOES
with HERB DRIZZLE

These tomatoes are wonderful with meats like pork, but even better on their own, crushed into a split baguette, with lots of wild rocket leaves.

20 CHERRY TOMATOES

1 tablespoon SUGAR

4 tablespoons VIRGIN OLIVE OIL

4 tablespoons CHOPPED FRESH OREGANO

SEA SALT AND FRESHLY GROUND BLACK PEPPER

TO SERVE

4 SMALL BAGUETTES, SPLIT LENGTHWAYS

4 tablespoons FRESHLY GRATED PARMESAN CHEESE

WILD ROCKET LEAVES

4 wooden skewers, soaked in water for at least 30 minutes

SERVES 4

Thread the tomatoes onto 4 soaked wooden skewers. Melt the sugar and oil in a saucepan and stir in the oregano, salt and pepper.

Put the skewers on a barbecue or under a hot grill and brush with the sugar-herb oil. Cook for 10 minutes or until the tomatoes are hot and the skin blistered.

Serve with meats or in split baguettes with Parmesan, rocket and a little of the sugar-herb oil.

CHAR-GRILLED MEDITERRANEAN VEGETABLES
with GARLIC and HERBS

I have always been worried about skewers threaded with meat and vegetables together. They cook at different speeds, so something is always bound to be badly cooked. Cook the vegetables on separate skewers, and part-cook the difficult ones, like pepper, onion (and bacon) first until almost tender, then this problem is solved.

OLIVE OIL, FOR BRUSHING

1 LARGE ONION, QUARTERED LENGTHWAYS THEN SEPARATED INTO PETALS

1 RED OR YELLOW PEPPER, HALVED AND DESEEDED

4 SLICES BACON OR SMOKED PANCETTA, CUT INTO 3 cm SQUARES

4 GARLIC CLOVES, HALVED

12 MUSHROOM CAPS, ABOUT 3 cm ACROSS

4 tablespoons CHOPPED FRESH TARRAGON, PARSLEY OR ROSEMARY

6 MEDIUM PLUM TOMATOES, HALVED AND DESEEDED

8 FRESH BAY LEAVES

SEA SALT AND FRESHLY GROUND BLACK PEPPER

4 metal or long bamboo skewers (if bamboo, soak in water for 30 minutes)

SERVES 4

Brush a heavy-based frying pan with the olive oil, add the onion petals and fry gently until softened and lightly browned. Remove to a plate. Put the pepper halves under the grill at a high heat and cook until the skins are blackened. Transfer to a saucepan, cover and let steam for 10 minutes. Add the bacon or pancetta and garlic to the frying pan and fry until lightly browned but still soft. Remove the bacon to the plate. Add the mushrooms to the pan and fry until lightly browned. Transfer the mushrooms to the plate and let cool a little. Leave the garlic in the frying pan.

Scrape the blistered skin off the peppers and cut the flesh into squares. Save any pepper juices and add to the frying pan with 1 tablespoon olive oil and the chopped herbs and garlic. Keep warm so the herbs and garlic infuse the oil.

Thread the mushrooms, tomato halves, onion petals, garlic pieces, bay leaves, bacon and pepper squares onto metal or soaked bamboo skewers. Brush with the oil and sprinkle with salt and freshly ground pepper. The dish can be prepared ahead to this point.

Put onto a preheated stove-top grill pan or barbecue rack or under a very hot grill and cook until toasty and brown on all sides, about 5–10 minutes, or until tender.

Remove to a serving platter and drizzle with the herbed oil mixture. Serve with roasted or barbecued meats or bean dishes, or in split baguettes or pita breads.

CHILLI SHRIMP BROCHETTES

Char-grilling prawns in their shells produces absolutely amazing flavour. Threading them onto skewers means you can turn the prawns easily without burning yourself. A hands-on dish!

12 LARGE UNCOOKED PRAWNS
OR 20 MEDIUM-SIZED

3–5 SPRING ONIONS, HALVED
LENGTHWAYS AND BLANCHED FOR
1 MINUTE IN BOILING WATER (OPTIONAL)

CHILLI LIME MARINADE

4 RED CHILLIES, DESEEDED AND CHOPPED

2–4 GARLIC CLOVES, CRUSHED

4 tablespoons PEANUT OIL

GRATED ZEST AND JUICE OF 3 LIMES

SEA SALT FLAKES

BREADCRUMBS, TOASTED IN A DRY
FRYING PAN (OPTIONAL)

*12–20 bamboo skewers, soaked in water
for at least 30 minutes*

SERVES 4

Push a toothpick into the neck of each prawn between head and shell and carefully hook out the black vein. Alternatively, cut down the back shell and draw out the vein. If preferred, remove the legs. You can also shell the prawns completely if you like.

To make the marinade, crush the chillies, garlic and salt using a fork or mortar and pestle. Put in a wide dish, add the oil, lime zest and juice and breadcrumbs, if using, and mix well. Put the prawns into the chilli mixture, pressing it into the backs if they have been cut.

For each prawn, insert a soaked bamboo skewer from the head end, pushing out the point where the back starts to curve. Tie the tail close to the chest with a blanched spring onion leaf, if using. Brush with marinade and char-grill on a barbecue or stove-top grill pan, or under a grill for 3–5 minutes on each side until the shells are brown and crispy and the flesh opaque.

FISH and SEAFOOD

To make the Chilli Onion Marmalade, put the onions, oil, bay leaf, chillies, if using, and sugar in a wide, heavy-based frying pan over a moderate heat. Cover and simmer over a low heat for about 15 minutes until the onions begin to soften (a pinch of salt will help the process). Stir every few minutes. Remove the lid, then add the vinegar, crème de cassis and allspice, if using. Cook gently, without stirring, until the onions have become translucent, about 15–20 minutes more. Remove, cool and transfer to a lidded container until ready to use. The marmalade will keep in the refrigerator for 1–2 days.

Trim the scallops if necessary and if the corals are still attached, prick them with a toothpick. Cut any large scallops in half crossways to make 2 discs. Heat the oil in a frying pan, add the spring onion pieces and pancetta and cook briefly on both sides until part-cooked but not crisp. Cool slightly.

Put a piece of spring onion on top of a scallop and wrap with a piece of pancetta. Secure with a soaked bamboo skewer, piercing the scallop through the diameter of the disc, if possible.

Put the skewers under a hot grill or on a barbecue at medium heat and cook until the scallops are opaque and the onions and bacon lightly browned at the edges. Do not overcook or the scallops will shrink and be tough.

Put the dressing ingredients in a wide, shallow bowl and beat with a fork. Add the salad leaves and toss to coat.

To serve, put small piles of leaves on 4 plates, add a spoonful of Chilli Onion Marmalade and divide the kebabs between the plates. Sprinkle with pepper and, if you like, drizzle a little dressing over each scallop before serving.

Scallops and bacon are a surprisingly delicious marriage of flavours. The Chilli Onion Marmalade is very good (omit the chilli if you like) and can be served with other recipes in this book.

SCALLOP and BACON KEBABS
with CHILLI ONION MARMALADE

12 MEDIUM SCALLOPS OR 8 LARGE

1 tablespoon OLIVE OIL

5–6 SPRING ONIONS, CUT INTO 3 cm LENGTHS

4–8 SLICES SMOKED PANCETTA

FRESHLY GROUND BLACK PEPPER

WILD ROCKET, BABY FRISÉE AND OTHER SALAD LEAVES, TO SERVE

LIGHT DRESSING

2 tablespoons OLIVE OIL

1 teaspoon WHITE RICE VINEGAR

1 tablespoon CHOPPED FRESH FLAT LEAF PARSLEY

SEA SALT AND FRESHLY GROUND BLACK PEPPER

CHILLI ONION MARMALADE

1 kg ONIONS, FINELY SLICED

4 tablespoons OLIVE OIL

1 FRESH BAY LEAF

4 LARGE CHILLIES, DESEEDED AND FINELY SLICED (OPTIONAL)

1 tablespoon SUGAR

A PINCH OF SALT (OPTIONAL)

1 tablespoon RED WINE VINEGAR

1 tablespoon CRÈME DE CASSIS (OPTIONAL)

¼ teaspoon GROUND ALLSPICE (OPTIONAL)

12–16 bamboo skewers, soaked in water for at least 30 minutes

SERVES 4

Wash the fish, pat dry and make 2–3 deep slashes into the thickest part on each side, cutting through to the bone. This will help the marinades penetrate the flesh.

Put 1 litre water in a flat-bottomed container, add the ingredients for the first marinade and stir. Add the fish and press down until well covered. Set aside for 30 minutes. (Indian cooks do not like very fishy flavours, so the first marination is designed to remove those flavours and to make the fish taste fresh and clean.)

To prepare the second marinade, put a layer of damp muslin in a strainer, add the yoghurt and set aside for 15 minutes to drain. (If you use thick yoghurt, you can omit this step.) Put the strained yoghurt into a bowl, beat in the egg yolk, then all the other ingredients.

Remove the fish from the first marinade and press with your fingers to wring out the liquid. Rub the yoghurt mixture all over the fish, pressing into the slashes in the sides. Cover and set aside to marinate in the refrigerator for 1 hour.

Push a long metal skewer into each fish, from head to tail. Roast for 8 minutes in a preheated oven at 200°C (400°F) Gas 6, under a hot grill, on a barbecue or in a tandoor oven (if you have one!). Remove from the heat and put in a heatproof bowl, pointed end down, for 3 minutes to let the moisture drip away. Baste with melted butter or ghee and roast for 3 minutes more, or until done.

Remove from the heat and serve with salad leaves, chunks of lemon or lime and finely sliced onion (cut it lengthways through the root for the authentic Indian look).

TANDOORI BARBECUED FISH

Chef Manjit Gil, from Delhi's famous Bokhara Restaurant, is perhaps the world's finest Indian chef. He says the secret to successful tandoor cooking is to cook the food in two stages, letting the meat or fish drain before the final stage.

4 WHOLE FISH SUCH AS SNAPPER OR POMFRET, ABOUT 500 g EACH, SCALED, CLEANED, WITH FINS TRIMMED

4 tablespoons MELTED BUTTER OR GHEE

FIRST MARINADE

2 tablespoons SALT

4 tablespoons WHITE VINEGAR (RICE OR MALT, NOT WINE)

2 tablespoons LEMON JUICE

SECOND MARINADE

5 tablespoons PLAIN YOGHURT

1 EGG YOLK

2.5 cm FRESH GINGER, PEELED AND GRATED

3 GARLIC CLOVES, CRUSHED

1 teaspoon AJWAIN (LOVAGE SEED) OR CELERY SEED (OPTIONAL)

1 tablespoon RED CHILLI POWDER

2 teaspoons GROUND TURMERIC

1 teaspoon SALT

1 teaspoon GARAM MASALA

1 tablespoon GRAM FLOUR (CHICKPEA FLOUR) OR CORNFLOUR

3 tablespoons FRESH CREAM

TO SERVE

FRESH SALAD LEAVES

4 LEMONS OR LIMES, CUT IN CHUNKS

1 RED ONION, SLICED LENGTHWAYS

4 long metal kebab skewers

SERVES 4

Monkfish is a firm-fleshed fish, which can take rough treatment such as barbecuing. But, like all fish, cook it just long enough for the flesh to become opaque. A smoky pancetta-style bacon will help hold it together and give extra pizzazz to its rather mild flavour. The sauce is gorgeous with many fish dishes.

MONKFISH BROCHETTES
with LEMON SOY BUTTER

4 tablespoons SUNFLOWER OR PEANUT OIL

8 THIN SLICES SMOKED PANCETTA, HALVED CROSSWAYS

500 g MONKFISH FILLETS

FRESH BAY LEAVES, HALVED LENGTHWAYS (OPTIONAL)

LEMON SOY BUTTER

4 tablespoons UNSALTED BUTTER

1 tablespoon SAKE OR VODKA

JUICE OF 1 LEMON

1 tablespoon TAMARI SOY SAUCE

3 cm FRESH GINGER, PEELED AND SLICED

2 GARLIC CLOVES, CRUSHED

TO SERVE

BABY SALAD LEAVES

BOILED NEW POTATOES

About 8 metal or bamboo skewers (if bamboo, soak in water for 30 minutes)

SERVES 4

Put the Lemon Soy Butter ingredients in a small pan and heat until frothing and well mixed.

Heat the oil in a frying pan, add the pancetta and fry gently until cooked but not crisp. Cool.

Cut the monkfish into 4 cm cubes. Brush with some of the oil, then wrap each cube in pancetta. Thread the parcels onto the skewers, alternating with pieces of bay leaf, if using.

Cook the brochettes at a high heat under a grill or on a barbecue, turning them over after 1–2 minutes, until the bacon is crispy and the fish just cooked, about 3 minutes in all. No longer, or the fish will overcook.

Serve the fish on a pile of baby salad leaves with the Lemon Soy Butter strained over the top and boiled new potatoes on the side.

SKEWERED TUNA SPIEDINI
with LEMON WEDGES, BAY LEAVES and CRACKED PEPPER

Make this chunky Mediterranean dish with tuna, swordfish or salmon, all of which have assertive flavours, strong enough to flourish with bay leaves and lemon. Tuna and salmon are best cooked slightly pink in the middle.

500 g TUNA STEAK, ABOUT 3 cm THICK

2 LEMONS, CUT IN 6 WEDGES EACH

16 SMALL FRESH BAY LEAVES

4 GARLIC CLOVES, CRUSHED

OLIVE OIL, FOR BASTING

SEA SALT AND COARSELY CRACKED BLACK PEPPER*

8–12 metal skewers, preferably double-pronged

SERVES 4

Cut the tuna steaks into cubes. Onto each skewer, thread 1 wedge of lemon, 2 bay leaves and 2 chunks of tuna.

Mix the garlic and oil in a bowl and brush all over the loaded skewers. Sprinkle with a little sea salt and lots of cracked black pepper.

Set aside for 10–30 minutes to develop the flavours, then char-grill at a high heat on a barbecue or under a grill. Cook on both sides until the fish is lightly browned, but still slightly pink in the middle.

Serve with red wine and lots of crusty bread.

Note: *To crack pepper, put whole peppercorns in a small mortar and crush with a pestle or the end of a rolling pin.*

This mixture can be cooked on other kinds of skewers, but lemongrass gives delicious flavour. Thai spice pastes can be bought ready-made, but if you can't find them, use the recipe given here.

LEMONGRASS STICKS

Put all the spice paste ingredients into a small blender and purée to a paste. Heat the oil in a small frying pan, add the paste and sauté for 5 minutes. Cool, then put into a bowl with the chicken or pork, coconut, chillies, sugar, lime zest, salt and pepper. Mix well.

Take 1–2 tablespoons of the mixture and press onto the end of the lemongrass or satay skewers. Wrap the exposed lemongrass handles in foil so they don't burn. Cook on a barbecue or under a hot grill until tender and golden, about 10 minutes on each side.

Serve in lettuce leaves, with *Nuóc Cham* dipping sauce.

2 tablespoons PEANUT OIL

600 g MINCED CHICKEN OR PORK

90 g DESICCATED COCONUT, SOAKED 30 MINUTES IN 250 ml BOILING WATER

1 LARGE RED CHILLI, DESEEDED AND FINELY CHOPPED

2 tablespoons BROWN SUGAR

GRATED ZEST OF 1 LIME

SEA SALT AND FRESHLY GROUND BLACK PEPPER

12 LEMONGRASS STALKS, WHOLE OR HALVED LENGTHWAYS, OR SATAY STICKS

ABOUT 12 SMALL LETTUCE LEAVES

NUÓC CHAM DIPPING SAUCE (PAGE 45), TO SERVE

SPICE PASTE

1 SHALLOT OR SMALL ONION, SLICED

6 GARLIC CLOVES, SLICED

2 RED CHILLIES, DESEEDED AND SLICED

3 cm FRESH GINGER, PEELED AND CHOPPED

1 teaspoon GROUND TURMERIC

2 teaspoon CORIANDER SEEDS, CRUSHED

1 teaspoon BLACK PEPPERCORNS, CRUSHED

6 ALMONDS, CRUSHED

1 tablespoon FISH SAUCE (OR SOY)

2 WHOLE CLOVES, CRUSHED

SERVES 4

Put all the yakitori sauce ingredients in a saucepan, stir, bring to the boil, boil hard for 3–5 minutes, then remove from the heat.

Char-grill the halved peppers until the skin blisters, then put in a saucepan and cover tightly. Let steam for 10 minutes, then scrape off the skin. Cut the peppers into 3 cm square pieces.

Char-grill or blanch the leeks or spring onions, then cut into 3 cm sections. Thread 2 quails' eggs onto 6 skewers and 2 mushrooms on another 6, with spring onion tops interspersed. Set aside.

Thread 8 skewers with chicken, grilled pepper, leek or spring onion. Char-grill all the skewers on a very hot barbecue or under a very hot grill (put the skewers as close to the heat as possible). Cook for 2 minutes on each side until the juices begin to flow, then transfer to the saucepan of sauce, sticks upwards.

Remove and cook for 1 minute on each side, then dip into the sauce again. Each time you dip, let excess sauce run off back into the pan. Grill again, until tender but not dried out.

Remove to a serving platter and serve sprinkled with pepper.

Though yakitori is traditionally made with green peppers, I prefer ripe ones, so use red or yellow instead. My supermarket sells a long, pointed kind, about 25 cm long, which are easy to peel. Many people don't pre-cook the vegetables, but the meat cooks long before they do, so I think it's important to give them a head-start. You can buy yakitori sauce from the supermarket, but home-made is better.

YAKITORI CHICKEN

4 LARGE RED OR YELLOW PEPPERS, HALVED AND DESEEDED

8 BABY LEEKS OR 12 SPRING ONIONS, HALVED LENGTHWAYS AND BLANCHED

8–12 BONED CHICKEN THIGHS, EACH CUT INTO 3 (ABOUT 3 cm CUBES)

FRESHLY GROUND BLACK PEPPER OR JAPANESE PEPPER

YAKITORI SAUCE

125 ml SAKE OR VODKA

200 ml DARK SOY SAUCE

3 tablespoons MIRIN (SWEET RICE WINE) OR SHERRY

2 tablespoons SUGAR

VEGETARIAN ALTERNATIVES

12 HARD-BOILED QUAILS' EGGS, SHELLED

12 CLOSE-CAPPED MUSHROOMS, ABOUT 3 cm DIAMETER

about 20 wooden or bamboo satay sticks, soaked in water for 30 minutes

SERVES 4

SPRING ONION CHICKEN SKEWERS

I think chicken thighs have more flavour than breasts. Use them for this simple, quick and easy Korean kebab.

Thread 1 piece of chicken and 1 piece of spring onion onto each skewer. Mix the marinade ingredients together in a flat, shallow dish. Add the skewers and turn to coat.

Cover and chill for 3 hours or overnight, turning in the marinade from time to time.

Cook on a barbecue or under a grill for about 5 minutes on each side or until done.

Variations

Beef is also good cooked in the same way. Cut 500 g steak into narrow strips, then thread one end of each strip onto a soaked bamboo skewer, alternately with the spring onions. If you like, add a splash of sake to the marinade. Marinate as in the main recipe, then grill until the meat is as rare or well-done as you prefer.

Prepare scallops in the same way, but omit the spring onion. Cook for a shorter time, just until the scallops become opaque, or they will shrink and become tough.

*Note: To make ginger purée, break fresh ginger into large pieces and soak in a bowl of water for about 30 minutes. Peel and purée in a blender, adding a splash of water if necessary. Freeze the purée in ice cube trays and use from frozen. One cube equals about 1 tablespoon purée.

8–12 CHICKEN THIGHS, SKINNED AND BONED, CUT INTO 3–4 PIECES EACH

ABOUT 12 SPRING ONIONS, CUT INTO 3 cm PIECES

GINGER MARINADE

2 GARLIC CLOVES, CRUSHED

2 tablespoons GINGER PURÉE, STORE-BOUGHT OR HOME-MADE*

3–4 tablespoons FISH SAUCE OR SOY SAUCE

1 tablespoon SESAME OIL

1 tablespoon SESAME SEEDS, TOASTED IN A DRY FRYING PAN

1 tablespoon SUGAR

1 tablespoon CORN OIL

24–36 wooden or bamboo satay sticks, soaked in water for 30 minutes

SERVES 4

SPATCHCOCKED POUSSINS
with ROASTED GARLIC, POTATOES and ONIONS

Spatchcocking (splitting a bird down the back then pressing it flat) produces a delicious, crisp dish with lots of flavour. People love eating this dish with their fingers, so provide lots of paper napkins or hot towels.

4 POUSSINS

2 teaspoons SEA SALT

2 tablespoons PAPRIKA

OLIVE OIL (SEE METHOD)

4 SPRIGS OF THYME

4 WHOLE HEADS OF GARLIC, TOPS SLICED OFF

12 SMALL RED POTATOES

2–3 RED ONIONS, CUT INTO WEDGES

8 flat metal kebab skewers

SERVES 4

Put the birds on a board, cut each one down either side of the backbone, then remove and discard it. Open out the carcasses, pressing down hard on the joints with the flat of your hand until they crack out flat. Fold the legs and wings close to the body. To keep the birds flat, thread 2 skewers crossways, running diagonally from the drumstick, through the breast, then the wing. Mix the salt with the paprika.

Put the birds, skin-side up, in a large roasting pan, brush with olive oil and sprinkle with the salt mixture. Add the thyme, garlic heads, potatoes and onion wedges and drizzle generously with oil. The dish can be prepared ahead to this point and kept in the fridge ready for last-minute cooking.

Preheat the oven to 200°C (400°F) Gas 6. Put the pan in the oven and roast for 15 minutes. Turn the birds over, reduce the heat to 190°C (375°F) Gas 5, and continue cooking for 15 minutes more. Turn them over again and cook until done, with crisp crunchy edges, about 45 minutes to 1 hour in total. Test with the point of another skewer – the juices should run clear with no trace of pink.

Serve the birds and vegetables on a large platter.

This delicious, authentic tandoori chicken was taught to me by Manjit Gill, one of the finest chefs in India, responsible for the North-west Frontier cooking in Delhi's Bokhara restaurant. Colour in all things has great significance in India, and though tandooris are often a lurid red or yellow, modern chefs, in India and the West, now avoid food colourings. Tandoori dishes are cooked on skewers, but these are removed before serving in a restaurant. If you cook them in small quantities, they can be served on the skewers instead.

TANDOORI CHICKEN

Cut the chicken into pieces about 2 x 3 cm. Pat dry. To make the first marinade, put the salt, ginger, garlic and vinegar in a bowl and stir well. Add the chicken, stir and set aside for 15 minutes.

Put the cheese, egg, chopped chillies, coriander, cornflour and half the cream in a blender or food processor and pulse to mix.

Remove the chicken from the first marinade and squeeze gently to remove excess moisture. Put into a clean bowl and add the blended second marinade. Turn in the mixture and massage it in with your fingers. Stir in the remaining cream and set aside for 30 minutes.

Fold the chicken pieces in half and thread onto the ends of soaked wooden skewers, 2–3 pieces per skewer. Cook for about 8 minutes on a barbecue, under a hot grill or in the oven at 200°C (400°F) Gas 6 until half-cooked (put a tray on the shelf underneath to collect the drippings).

Remove the skewers from the heat and set them upright in a bowl for 5 minutes so excess moisture can drain away.

Remove the chicken pieces from the skewers, unfold them and re-thread them flat, leaving a gap between the pieces. Baste with melted butter or oil and return to the grill or oven until done, about 8 minutes. Sprinkle with the juice of 1 lemon and serve with finely sliced onions (salt them first to soften), torn salad leaves and the remaining lemon, cut in wedges.

750 g BONELESS, SKINLESS CHICKEN

MELTED BUTTER OR OIL, FOR BRUSHING

FIRST MARINADE

1 tablespoon SALT

2.5 cm FRESH GINGER, PEELED AND GRATED

3 GARLIC CLOVES, CRUSHED

2 tablespoons WHITE VINEGAR (RICE OR MALT, NOT WINE)

SECOND MARINADE

5 tablespoons GRATED PROCESSED CHEESE OR MILD CHEDDAR

1 SMALL EGG, BEATEN

4 GREEN CHILLIES, DESEEDED AND CHOPPED

1 LARGE BUNCH FRESH CORIANDER, CHOPPED (ABOUT 10 g)

1 tablespoon CORNFLOUR

100 ml SINGLE CREAM

TO SERVE

2 LEMONS

FINELY SLICED RED ONION

SALAD LEAVES

8 long wooden or bamboo skewers, soaked in water for 30 minutes

SERVES 4

Thais do the world's best stick food. From the finest restaurant to the simplest street hawker's stall, they seem incapable of turning out anything but great food.

THAI CHICKEN SATAYS

Thread the chicken strips, zig-zag fashion, onto soaked satay sticks. Mix the marinade ingredients in a bowl, then add the sticks, turning them until well coated. Chill for 1 hour, turning occasionally.

To make the sauce, put the peanuts, if using, in a pan and toast until light brown. Crush coarsely and reserve. Soak the dried chillies in boiling water for 30 minutes, then transfer to a spice mill (clean coffee grinder) or blender and add the shallots or onion, garlic, candlenuts or almonds, and lemongrass or lemon juice. Work to a paste.

Heat the corn oil in a wok or frying pan, add the chilli mixture and sauté gently for 5 minutes, stirring several times. Add the coconut milk and simmer, stirring constantly (keep stirring, and don't cover the pan, or the coconut milk will curdle). Add the tamarind paste or lime juice, sugar, salt and peanuts or peanut butter. Simmer for about 2 minutes, then cool a little and serve in a bowl, topped with coriander leaves.

Remove the chicken satays from the marinade and cook on a barbecue or under a grill at medium heat for 2 minutes on each side, or until cooked through and lightly browned at the edges.

Note: If the sauce sits for any length of time, you may need to thin it a little with hot water before serving.

4 LARGE BONELESS CHICKEN BREASTS, SKINNED AND CUT CROSSWAYS INTO 5–10 mm STRIPS

3 tablespoons CORN OIL

COCONUT MARINADE

2 tablespoons THAI 7-SPICE OR 1 tablespoon CHINESE 5-SPICE

1 tablespoon BROWN SUGAR

1 tablespoon LIME JUICE

2–3 cm FRESH GINGER, PEELED AND GRATED

1 tablespoon FISH SAUCE

125 ml CANNED COCONUT MILK

SATAY SAUCE

125 ml UNSALTED PEANUTS OR PEANUT BUTTER

5 DRIED RED CHILLIES

8 SMALL SHALLOTS OR 1 MILD ONION

1 GARLIC CLOVE, CRUSHED

4 CANDLENUTS OR 8 ALMONDS, COARSELY CHOPPED

1 STALK LEMONGRASS, FINELY CHOPPED, OR JUICE OF 1 LEMON

2 tablespoons PEANUT OIL

250 ml CANNED COCONUT MILK

2 teaspoons TAMARIND PASTE OR JUICE OF 1 LIME

1 teaspoon BROWN SUGAR

SALT

A FEW CORIANDER LEAVES, CHOPPED, TO SERVE

20 wooden or bamboo satay sticks, soaked in water for 30 minutes

SERVES 4

Satays are popular South-east Asian snacks, and each country has its favourite accompaniments. *Nuóc Cham* is Vietnamese, Satay Sauce is Thai, Malay or Indonesian. (*Satay* means 'three'.)

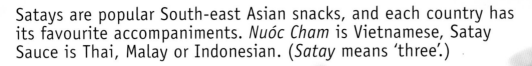

CHICKEN SATAYS
MARINATED in GINGER and TAMARIND

Mix the tamarind marinade ingredients together in a jug or bowl.

Cut the chicken into slices, 1 cm wide, then cut those slices into strips, 1 cm wide. Thread them, zig-zag fashion, onto soaked wooden or bamboo skewers. Put the skewers in a flat, shallow dish and pour over the marinade. Set aside for 30 minutes.

When ready to cook, drain the satays, pour the marinade into a saucepan, bring to boiling point, then simmer, stirring, for 15 minutes. Cook the satays on a barbecue or under a medium-hot grill until cooked through.

Serve with the hot tamarind marinade and *Nuóc Cham* or Satay Sauce. (A traditional Vietnamese serving treatment is to serve with a 'table salad' of shredded carrot, mint and Asian basil leaves, soaked rice noodles and lettuce leaves for wrapping.)

4 CHICKEN BREASTS, SKINNED
AND BONED

NUÓC CHAM (PAGE 45) OR SATAY SAUCE
(PAGES 37 OR 53), TO SERVE

TAMARIND MARINADE

1 tablespoon GINGER PURÉE (PAGE 30)
OR 2 cm FRESH GINGER, PEELED
AND GRATED

3 GARLIC CLOVES, CRUSHED

125 ml FISH SAUCE OR SOY SAUCE

2 tablespoons TAMARIND PASTE OR
JUICE OF 2 LIMES

200 ml COCONUT MILK

2 tablespoons PEANUT OIL

*12–20 long wooden or
bamboo satay sticks,
soaked in water for
30 minutes*

SERVES 4

I prefer duck breasts with the crispy skin still attached, but feel free to discard it before cooking if you like.

DUCK BREAST SATAYS
with PEPPER LEMON MARINADE

Cut the duck breasts diagonally into strips about 5–10 mm wide. Thread onto soaked bamboo sticks or metal skewers. Mix the remaining ingredients together in a bowl, add the skewers, turn to coat and let marinate for 30 minutes. Drain and cook over a high heat until done to your liking (duck is nicer a little rare). Meanwhile, bring the marinade mixture to the boil, simmer for 5 minutes, then transfer to a dipping bowl. Serve the satays with the dip.

Mediterranean alternative

Brush the duck skewers with red pesto before grilling, then serve as part of a plate of tapas, with a glass of ice-cold sherry.

2 LARGE DUCK BREASTS, WITH OR WITHOUT SKIN

125 ml SWEET SOY SAUCE, SUCH AS INDONESIAN KECAP MANIS

½ teaspoon GROUND CORIANDER

1 teaspoon FRESHLY GROUND BLACK PEPPER

JUICE OF 1 LEMON

2 MEDIUM SHALLOTS, FINELY SLICED

12–20 bamboo satay sticks, soaked in water for 30 minutes, or metal skewers

SERVES 4

500 g TURKEY ESCALOPES

BABY SALAD LEAVES, TO SERVE

CHILLI MARINADE

200 ml RED WINE

JUICE OF ½ LEMON OR 1 LIME

100 ml OLIVE OIL

1 RED CHILLI, DESEEDED AND DICED

2 GARLIC CLOVES, CRUSHED

1 ONION, VERY FINELY CHOPPED

1 teaspoon SALT

1 tablespoon SUGAR

1 tablespoon COARSELY CRUSHED
BLACK PEPPER

PAPAYA SALSA

1 SMALL RIPE PAPAYA, PEELED
AND DESEEDED

1 RED PEPPER

1 RED CHILLI, DESEEDED AND DICED

1 tablespoon GRATED FRESH GINGER

6 BABY CORNICHONS, FINELY SLICED

6 tablespoons TORN FRESH
CORIANDER LEAVES

GRATED ZEST AND JUICE OF 3 LIMES

SEA SALT AND FRESHLY GROUND
BLACK PEPPER

8 metal kebab skewers

SERVES 4

A recipe filled with New World flavours. Turkey is a healthy meat that deserves to be served other than at Christmas time. The fruity salsa is full of sweet flavours and spicy notes of chilli and ginger – serve it also with other dishes in this book. Delicious!

CHILLI TURKEY KEBABS
with PAPAYA SALSA

Put the marinade ingredients in a bowl and beat with a fork. Cut the turkey into 2–3 cm cubes, add to the marinade, cover and chill overnight.

When ready to cook, drain the turkey and thread onto metal skewers. Put the marinade in a small saucepan and bring to the boil. Simmer for 5 minutes and reserve.

To make the salsa, cut the papaya into 1 cm dice. Peel the pepper with a vegetable peeler (don't worry if you don't get all the peel), then deseed and cut into 1 cm dice. Put in a small serving bowl, add the other salsa ingredients and mix well.

Preheat a barbecue or grill to medium hot and cook the turkey skewers about 7–8 cm from the heat for 3–4 minutes, turning and basting the meat with the reserved marinade, or until the turkey is cooked all the way through.

Serve with a few salad leaves and the salsa. Warmed soft flour tortillas would also be a delicious accompaniment.

SINGAPORE PORK SATAYS

In South-east Asia, satays are served as snacks, or with other dishes as part of a meal, not as a main course. For a party or barbecue, prepare a selection of different satays and sauces and serve them all together.

1 kg BONELESS PORK LOIN

1 tablespoon CORIANDER SEEDS

½ teaspoon GROUND TURMERIC

1 teaspoon SALT

1 tablespoon BROWN SUGAR

1 STALK LEMONGRASS, FINELY SLICED

5 SMALL SHALLOTS, FINELY CHOPPED

125 ml SUNFLOWER OR PEANUT OIL

TO SERVE

1 CUCUMBER, QUARTERED LENGTHWAYS, DESEEDED, THEN SLICED CROSSWAYS INTO CHUNKS

DIPPING SAUCE, SUCH AS SATAY SAUCE (PAGE 37 OR 53), NUÓC CHAM (PAGE 45) OR CHOPPED CHILLI MIXED WITH SOY OR FISH SAUCE

20 wooden or bamboo satay sticks, soaked in water for 30 minutes

SERVES 4

Cut the pork across the grain into 2 cm slices, then into cubes.

Heat the coriander seeds in a dry frying pan until aromatic. Put into a spice mill (or clean coffee grinder) and grind to a powder. Put into a large bowl, then add the turmeric, salt and sugar.

Put the finely sliced lemongrass and shallots in the spice mill or a blender and work to a paste (add a little water if necessary). Add to the bowl and stir well. Stir in 2 tablespoons of the oil.

Add the cubes of meat and turn to coat in the mixture. Cover and marinate in the refrigerator for 2 hours or overnight.

When ready to cook, thread cubes of pork onto soaked satay sticks, 2 on each, leaving a little space between the pieces. Brush with oil and cook over medium heat on a barbecue or under a grill until done. (Pork must be cooked right through – and not at too high a heat, or it will be tough.)

Thread a piece of cucumber onto the end of each skewer and serve with dipping sauce.

PORK, LAMB and BEEF

Put the pork, garlic, lemongrass, coriander, chillies, brown sugar, fish sauce and egg in a food processor and work to a paste. Chill for at least 30 minutes.

Take 1–2 tablespoons of the mixture and, using wet hands, form into a ball. Repeat until all the mixture has been used. Press a soaked chopstick or skewer through the middle of each ball and thread 2–3 balls onto each stick. Pat until snug, then chill.

To make the *Nuóc Cham*, work the garlic, chilli and sugar to a purée in a spice mill (clean coffee grinder) or with a mortar and pestle. Add the chopped lime and any collected juice, then purée again. Stir in the fish sauce and about 125 ml water. Reserve.

Toast the peanuts for serving in a dry frying pan, then crush coarsely and reserve. Soak the noodles in hot water for about 15 minutes, drain, then boil for 1 minute. Drain and reserve.

Cook the pork balls on a barbecue or under a hot grill until cooked right through (break one open to check). Serve, sprinkled with chopped peanuts, with a 'table salad' of lettuce, mint and basil. To eat, remove from the sticks, wrap in lettuce, add noodles, carrots, peanuts and herbs, then roll up and dip in *Nuóc Cham*.

Note: *Fish sauce is delicious and traditional. If unavailable, use soy sauce diluted with water.*

VIETNAMESE PORK BALL
BROCHETTES

These traditional kebabs are called brochettes, the result of the French colonial period, but the flavours are distinctly Vietnamese, especially the herbs, salad and *Nuóc Cham* – the delicious, piquant, salty, spicy condiment used as an all-purpose dipping sauce.

500 g MINCED PORK, WITH SOME FAT

4 GARLIC CLOVES, CRUSHED

2 STALKS LEMONGRASS, FINELY SLICED

1 BUNCH CORIANDER, CHOPPED

2 RED CHILLIES, DESEEDED AND DICED

1 tablespoon BROWN SUGAR

1 tablespoon FISH SAUCE*

1 EGG, BEATEN

NUÓC CHAM

2 GARLIC CLOVES, CRUSHED

1 RED CHILLI, DESEEDED AND CHOPPED

1 tablespoon SUGAR

½ LIME, DESEEDED AND CHOPPED (PEEL INCLUDED)

1½ tablespoons FISH SAUCE*

TO SERVE

4–8 tablespoons CHOPPED PEANUTS

30 g RICE STICK NOODLES

16–20 SMALL LETTUCE LEAVES

LEAVES FROM 1 BUNCH FRESH BASIL

LEAVES FROM 1 BUNCH FRESH MINT

2 CARROTS, GRATED INTO STRIPS

12–16 short wooden chopsticks or bamboo skewers, soaked in water for 30 minutes

SERVES 4

AFGHAN LAMB KEBABS
with GINGER, RED WINE and BAY LEAVES

All through Pakistan and Afghanistan, restaurants and roadside barbecue stalls produce iron skewers of lamb, chicken and occasionally beef. The skewers are terrifying – about a metre long – and served in great bundles in the middle of the table with huge piles of delicious fresh naan bread. Muslim cooks wouldn't use wine or the ginger, for that matter, but I think it improves the flavour enormously. Beef is also good cooked this way.

1 SMALL LEG OF LAMB

6 tablespoons GINGER PURÉE* (PAGE 30), OR 5 cm FRESH GINGER, GRATED

½ BOTTLE RED WINE, OR TO COVER

2 FRESH BAY LEAVES, BRUISED

GHEE, MUSTARD OIL, OR OLIVE OIL, FOR BRUSHING

SEA SALT

WARM NAAN BREAD, TO SERVE

CUCUMBER RAITA (OPTIONAL)

1 CUCUMBER, DESEEDED, SLICED, SALTED, THEN RINSED AND PATTED DRY

1 TOMATO, DESEEDED AND DICED

1 ONION, FINELY SLICED

125 ml PLAIN YOGHURT

SALT AND FRESHLY GROUND BLACK PEPPER

12 long metal kebab skewers

SERVES 4

Ask the butcher to cut the leg of lamb across the bone into thick slices, about 3 cm wide. Remove and discard the central bone from each slice, then cut the meat into 3 cm cubes.

Put in a bowl, add the ginger and turn to coat. Add the wine and bay leaves, cover, then marinate in the refrigerator for 1 hour or up to 2 days.

Remove from the marinade and pat dry. Thread onto metal skewers, brush with melted ghee or oil and sprinkle with sea salt.

Mix the raita ingredients together in a small bowl and set aside.

Cook the kebabs on a barbecue or under a very hot grill for about 5 minutes on each side, until the meat is crisp and brown outside and still pink inside. Serve with the raita and naan bread.

Note: Ginger purée is sold in supermarkets. To make your own, see the recipe note on page 30.

What did we do before food processors? Spent all day grinding things like the meat for these kibbehs (now a work of seconds in the wonder machine). I use the small part for chopping onions, then tip them into the larger part to mix them with the meat.

MIDDLE EASTERN KIBBEH KEBABS
with TABBOULEH, HOUMMUS and PITA

Put the onions in a small food processor (these chop onions better than the large ones). Pulse to the equivalent of coarsely grated. Add the parsley and chop again. Transfer to a large processor, with the lamb mince, spices and seasoning and pulse to a smooth paste.

Pat 16 flat metal skewers completely dry. Take a ball of mixture, about 2 tablespoons, and put on the end of the skewer, about 2 cm from the end. Press it along the skewer to make an oval or cylinder about 10 cm long. (Since the mixture can easily fall off the skewers, try putting the skewers inside a hinged grill rack.)

Cook under a grill or on a barbecue at the highest heat. Grill for about 2 minutes on each side until crisp on the outside and tender inside.

Put on a large serving platter with a pile of warmed pita bread beside and separate bowls of sliced onion, salad leaves, hoummus and yoghurt mixed with dried mint, if using. (Traditionally, the meat is pulled off the skewers with the bread.)

2 ONIONS, QUARTERED

A LARGE HANDFUL OF PARSLEY, STALKS REMOVED (100 g)

500 g LAMB MINCE

1/2 teaspoon GROUND CINNAMON

1/2 teaspoon GROUND SAFFRON

SEA SALT AND COARSELY CRUSHED BLACK PEPPER

TO SERVE

PITA BREAD

SLICED RED ONION

GREEN SALAD LEAVES

HOUMMUS

PLAIN YOGHURT

1 teaspoon DRIED MINT (OPTIONAL)

about 16 flat-sided metal skewers

hinged metal grill rack, oiled (optional)

SERVES 4

1 SMALL LEG OF LAMB

GARLIC MARINADE

6 GARLIC CLOVES, CRUSHED

3 tablespoons EXTRA-VIRGIN OLIVE OIL

GRATED ZEST AND JUICE OF 1 LEMON

A PINCH OF FRESHLY GROUND CINNAMON

A PINCH OF FRESHLY GROUND CLOVES

SEA SALT AND COARSELY CRUSHED
BLACK PEPPER

TO SERVE

WARMED LAVASH OR VILLAGE BREAD

TABBOULEH SALAD

HOUMMUS

CHILLI SAUCE (OPTIONAL)

CHOPPED FRESH TOMATO

*8 metal or bamboo skewers (if bamboo,
soak in water for 30 minutes*

SERVES 4

Ask the butcher to cut the lamb into slices across the bone, about 2.5 cm wide. Remove the bone from the middle and separate the meat across the natural separations. Cut into cubes.

Mix the garlic marinade ingredients in a bowl, then add the lamb and turn to coat well. Cover and leave for 2 hours or overnight in the refrigerator. Turn occasionally if possible.

Remove the lamb from the marinade and thread onto metal skewers. Barbecue or grill at high heat for about 5–7 minutes on each side.

Serve rolled up in warmed lavash or village bread with tabbouleh salad, hoummus, chilli sauce, if using, and chopped tomatoes.

Greek and Lebanese Australians make these wraps with char-grilled fillets from the loin of the lamb. This can be a little expensive outside lamb-growing areas, so I have used slices from the leg. Village bread or lavash are thin scarf-like sheets of flatbread. Use pita if unavailable.

SOUVLAKI LAMB
with HOUMMUS and TABBOULEH SALAD,
WRAPPED in WARMED VILLAGE BREAD

This marinade and sauce can be used for other satay skewers such as chicken, duck and (not very Indonesian) pork. Some chillies are milder than others, so choose the variety and number of chillies to suit the palates of your guests. You can also use the satay sauce on page 37.

INDONESIAN BEEF SATAYS
with PEANUT SATAY SAUCE

Cut the beef crossways into thin strips, about 5 mm thick and 5 cm long.

To make the coconut marinade, mix the coconut milk, lime juice, chilli, lemongrass or lemon, garlic, coriander, cumin, cardamom, fish sauce, lime zest and sugar in a bowl. Add the beef strips and stir to coat. Cover and chill for 2 hours or overnight to develop the flavours.

To make the Satay Sauce, grind the peanuts in a blender or food processor until coarse. Heat the oil in a wok, add the garlic, chillies and onion and stir-fry until golden. Add peanuts, sugar, lime juice, coconut milk and soy sauce. Bring to the boil and simmer, stirring, until thickened.

Drain the beef, discarding the marinade. Thread the beef, zig-zag fashion, onto soaked wooden or bamboo skewers and cook under a hot grill or in a frying pan (brushed with a film of peanut oil) until browned and tender. Serve, sprinkled with peanuts, if using, and satay sauce.

*Note: The sauce recipe makes about 500 ml, which is enough for 2–3 other kinds of satays to be served at the same meal.

500 g BEEF STEAK

125 ml PEANUTS, CRUSHED, TO SERVE (OPTIONAL)

COCONUT MARINADE

125 ml CANNED COCONUT MILK

JUICE OF 2 LIMES (ABOUT 75 ml)

2 FRESH RED CHILLIES, FINELY CHOPPED

3 STALKS LEMONGRASS OR 1 LEMON, FINELY CHOPPED

3 GARLIC CLOVES, CRUSHED

2 teaspoons GROUND CORIANDER

1 teaspoon GROUND CUMIN

1 teaspoon GROUND CARDAMOM

2 tablespoons FISH SAUCE

GRATED ZEST OF 1 KAFFIR LIME

1 teaspoon SUGAR

SATAY SAUCE*

250 g ROASTED PEANUTS

1 teaspoon PEANUT OIL

1 GARLIC CLOVE, CRUSHED

2 RED CHILLIES, DESEEDED AND DICED

1 ONION, FINELY SLICED

1 tablespoon BROWN SUGAR

1 teaspoon LIME JUICE

250 ml CANNED COCONUT MILK

1 tablespoon SWEETENED SOY SAUCE, SUCH AS INDONESIAN KECAP MANIS

12 long bamboo skewers, soaked in water for 30 minutes

SERVES 4

750 g SKIRT STEAK, CUT INTO
2.5 cm CUBES

2 RED ONIONS, CUT INTO WEDGES

2 RED PEPPERS, DESEEDED AND CUT
INTO 2.5 cm SQUARES

CORN OIL, FOR BRUSHING

FAJITA MARINADE

1½ tablespoons OLIVE OIL

1½ tablespoons LIME JUICE

A PINCH OF SEA SALT FLAKES

2 teaspoons TABASCO OR CHILLI OIL

½ teaspoon CRUSHED CHILLIES

4 GARLIC CLOVES, CRUSHED

TOMATO SALSA

3 TOMATOES, DESEEDED AND DICED

1 SHALLOT, CHOPPED

2 tablespoons CHOPPED
FRESH CORIANDER

JUICE OF 1 LIME

1 tablespoon CHOPPED
JALAPEÑO CHILLI

SALT AND FRESHLY GROUND
BLACK PEPPER

TO SERVE

DRIED CHILLI FLAKES

12 FLOUR TORTILLAS, WARMED

GUACAMOLE

SPRIGS OF CORIANDER

12 metal kebab skewers

hinged metal grill rack, oiled (optional)

SERVES 4

Mix the marinade ingredients in a flat, shallow dish, add the meat cubes and turn to coat. Cover and chill for at least 2 hours or overnight.

Brush the onions and peppers with oil and put on a heated stove-top grill pan. Cook until browned on all sides. Mix the salsa ingredients in a small bowl. Thread the meat onto half the skewers and the pepper and onion onto the remaining skewers. Put the skewers in a hinged grill rack and cook on a barbecue or under a grill until crispy brown. Sprinkle with chilli flakes.

Serve with warmed tortillas, guacamole, coriander and salsa, either assembled or in separate dishes for guests to make up to their own taste.

In Spanish, a *fajita* is a belt or band – in food terms, fajitas are marinades, usually applied to large pieces of skirt steak, but also wonderful with skewers and with other ingredients such as chicken or seafood.

BEEF FAJITAS
with CHILLI SPRINKLE

I grew up on a pineapple farm and, to us professionals, the dinky little discs you see in cans or in restaurants were for the birds! Pineapples come with their own, albeit rather prickly, handle. You just slice off the skin with a machete, hold the fruit by the top and munch away. If we were being very civilized, the peeled pineapples would be cut into wedges like these. Perfect for cooking, juicing or eating daintily with a knife and fork.

PINEAPPLE STICKS
with SUGAR-LIME SAUCE

Put the Sugar-lime Sauce ingredients in a saucepan, bring to the boil and stir until the sugar dissolves.

To make the Coconut Cream, beat the cream with the icing sugar until soft peaks form, then fold in the coconut cream, if using.

Cut the pineapple quarters into 2–3 wedges lengthways. If preferred, slice off the core sections, then cut each wedge into slices about 1 cm thick. Thread long metal skewers through each wedge and brush with the sugar-lime mixture.

Cook under a searing hot grill or on a barbecue until the fruit is tinged with dark brown. Serve drizzled with any leftover sauce, accompanied by the whipped coconut cream.

1 PINEAPPLE, PEELED AND QUARTERED LENGTHWAYS (REMOVE THE PRICKLY EYES WITH THE POINT OF A KNIFE)

SUGAR-LIME SAUCE

JUICE OF 1 FRESH LIME (2 tablespoons)

100 g BROWN SUGAR

WHIPPED COCONUT CREAM

250 ml DOUBLE CREAM

2 tablespoons ICING SUGAR

2 tablespoons CANNED COCONUT CREAM (OPTIONAL)

8 metal kebab skewers

SERVES 4

SWEET THINGS

To make the batter, beat the egg in a small bowl with 150 ml cold water. Sift the flour into a second bowl and gradually stir in the egg mixture to form a smooth batter.

Peel the bananas and cut them at an angle crossways into pieces about 2.5 cm long.

Half fill a large bowl with ice cubes and cold water and set beside the stove. Film a serving plate with oil and set beside the water.

To make the Sugar Syrup, put the oil in a saucepan with the sugar and 3 tablespoons water. Heat, stirring, until the sugar dissolves, then heat gently, without stirring, until the mixture reaches hard crack stage – 150°C (300°F) on a sugar thermometer or when a drop of syrup, dropped into the bowl of water, hardens instantly.

Fill a wok one-third full of the oil and heat to 190°C (375°F) or until a piece of bread browns in 30 seconds.

Stick soaked cocktail sticks or chip forks* into the banana pieces, dip the fruit into the batter, then put into the hot oil and cook for 1 minute. (Work in batches of 4–6.) Remove from the oil with a slotted spoon and dip into the sugar syrup, holding the stick with tongs. Sprinkle with sesame seeds, then immediately drop them, one by one, into the iced water. The syrup hardens instantly into a crackly glaze. Transfer to a serving plate and serve sprinkled with icing sugar or more sesame seeds.

*Note: Alternatively, the sticks may be inserted after cooking.

3–4 JUST-RIPE BANANAS

3 tablespoons SESAME SEEDS, TOASTED IN A DRY FRYING PAN

PEANUT OR SUNFLOWER OIL, FOR FRYING

4 tablespoons ICING SUGAR, FOR DUSTING (OPTIONAL)

FRITTER BATTER

1 EGG

125 g PLAIN FLOUR

SUGAR SYRUP

1 tablespoon PEANUT OIL

125 g SUGAR

about 20 wooden cocktail sticks or chip forks, soaked in water for 30 minutes

SERVES 4

Hugely popular, this traditional Chinese dish depends for its success on the sugar syrup staying at precisely the same temperature. Use a sugar thermometer (available from good kitchen shops) to help you – and remember, practice makes perfect.

CHINESE BANANA FRITTERS

When I was little, toffee apples were always very red and crisp – my favourite was the tiny, white-fleshed Lady in the Snow. Pick one of the small apples now sold in supermarkets – you get more toffee for your apple! Use wooden chopsticks to make skewers.

TOFFEE APPLES

8–12 SMALL RED APPLES

500 g BROWN SUGAR

50 g UNSALTED BUTTER

2 tablespoons VINEGAR

1 tablespoon GOLDEN SYRUP OR CORN SYRUP

a baking tray, greased

8–12 short wooden chopsticks

SERVES 8–12

Soak the apples in cold water for 10–30 minutes. Rinse, then dry completely with kitchen paper.

Put the sugar in a saucepan with the butter, vinegar, golden syrup and ⅔ cup water. Heat gently, stirring, until the sugar dissolves. Boil hard for about 5 minutes, stirring occasionally to stop the mixture sticking. Continue boiling until the mixture reaches hard ball stage – 123°C (250°F) on a sugar thermometer or when a teaspoon of syrup, dropped into cold water, hardens instantly into a ball. If it doesn't, continue boiling until it does.

Push thick wooden sticks, such as chopsticks, into the apples, then dip them into the toffee, twirling them around for a few seconds. Remove and leave on the greased baking tray, sticks upward, until the toffee hardens – about 10 minutes. Serve immediately, or wrap the toffee apples in cellophane and tie with ribbons.

250 ml MILK

3 EGG YOLKS

125 g SUGAR

250 ml DOUBLE OR WHIPPING CREAM

FRUIT FLAVOURINGS:

2–3 RIPE MANGOES, PEELED AND STONED

JUICE OF 1 SMALL LEMON

2 tablespoons CASTER SUGAR

1 PUNNET STRAWBERRIES, ABOUT
325 ml QUARTERED

8 RIPE APRICOTS, HALVED AND STONED

12–24 lollipop sticks

MAKES ABOUT 12 LARGE OR 24 SMALL

You can buy plastic lollipop moulds with attached plastic sticks. I prefer wooden sticks, then you can use any kind of container as a mould, ranging from eggcups to timbales or small plastic cups.

ICE CREAM LOLLIPOPS

If using mangoes, purée the flesh in a blender with the lemon juice and sugar. Chill. If using strawberries or apricots, put in a saucepan with the lemon juice, sugar and ¼ cup water, bring to the boil and simmer until soft. Strain into a bowl and chill.

To make the ice cream, heat the milk to just below boiling point. Put the egg yolks in a bowl and beat until creamy. Beat in a quarter of the hot milk, then the remaining milk, a little at a time. Stir in the sugar and transfer to a bowl set over simmering water. Cook, stirring, until the mixture coats the back of a spoon. Do not let boil. Remove from the heat, dip the bowl into cold water, then cool.

Stir in the cream, add your choice of fruit, then churn, in batches if necessary.* Spoon into lollipop moulds and insert the sticks. If using makeshift moulds, put a lollipop stick in the middle.

Freeze, then serve as required to greedy small people.

__Note:__ Alternatively, part-freeze in a shallow metal pan, whizz in a food processor, then freeze again.

INDEX